First Holy Communion

Guest Book

Guest of Honor: _____

Date: _____

Name:

✝ _____

✝ _____

✝ _____

✝ _____

Message:

[ ]

[ ]

[ ]

[ ]

Name:

✝ _____

✝ _____

✝ _____

✝ _____

Message:

Name:

Message:

✝ _____

✝ _____

✝ _____

✝ _____

Name:

Message:

✝ _____

✝ _____

✝ _____

✝ _____

Name:

Message:

✝ _____

✝ _____

✝ _____

✝ _____

Name:

✝ _____

✝ _____

✝ _____

✝ _____

Message:

Name:

Message:

✝ _____

✝ _____

✝ _____

✝ _____

Name:

✝ _____

✝ _____

✝ _____

✝ _____

Message:

Name:

Message:

✝ _____

✝ _____

✝ _____

✝ _____

Name:

✝ _____

✝ _____

✝ _____

✝ _____

Message:

Name:

✝ _____

✝ _____

✝ _____

✝ _____

Message:

Name:

✝ _____

✝ _____

✝ _____

✝ _____

Message:

Name:

Message:

✝ _____

✝ _____

✝ _____

✝ _____

Name:

Message:

† _____

† _____

† _____

† _____

Name:

✝ _____

✝ _____

✝ _____

✝ _____

Message:

Name:

✝ _____

✝ _____

✝ _____

✝ _____

Message:

Name:

✝ _____

✝ _____

✝ _____

✝ _____

Message:

```




```

```




```

```




```

```




```

Name:

† _____

† _____

† _____

† _____

Message:

Name:

Message:

†
_____

†
_____

†
_____

†
_____

Name:

✝ _____

✝ _____

✝ _____

✝ _____

Message:

Name:

Message:

Name:

✝ _____

✝ _____

✝ _____

✝ _____

Message:

Name:

✝ _____

✝ _____

✝ _____

✝ _____

Message:

```
┌──────────────────┐
│                  │
│                  │
│                  │
└──────────────────┘
```

```
┌──────────────────┐
│                  │
│                  │
│                  │
└──────────────────┘
```

```
┌──────────────────┐
│                  │
│                  │
│                  │
└──────────────────┘
```

```
┌──────────────────┐
│                  │
│                  │
│                  │
└──────────────────┘
```

Name:

Message:

✝ _____

✝ _____

✝ _____

✝ _____

Name:

Message:

†

†

†

†

Name:

✝ _____

✝ _____

✝ _____

✝ _____

Message:

Name:

✝ _____

✝ _____

✝ _____

✝ _____

Message:

Name:

✝ _____

✝ _____

✝ _____

✝ _____

Message:

Name:

✝ _____

✝ _____

✝ _____

✝ _____

Message:

Name:

†
_____

†
_____

†
_____

†
_____

Message:

Name:

†_____

†_____

†_____

†_____

Message:

Name:

Message:

✝ _____

✝ _____

✝ _____

✝ _____

Name:

Message:

†_____

†_____

†_____

†_____

Name:

† _____

† _____

† _____

† _____

Message:

Name:

† _____

† _____

† _____

† _____

Message:

Name:

✝ _____

✝ _____

✝ _____

✝ _____

Message:

Name:

Message:

✝ _____

✝ _____

✝ _____

✝ _____

Name:

✝ _____

✝ _____

✝ _____

✝ _____

Message:

Name:

✝ _____

✝ _____

✝ _____

✝ _____

Message:

Name:

✝ _____

✝ _____

✝ _____

✝ _____

Message:

Name:

Message:

Name:

Message:

✝ _____

✝ _____

✝ _____

✝ _____

Name:

✝ _____

✝ _____

✝ _____

✝ _____

Message:

Name:

†_____

†_____

†_____

†_____

Message:

[ ]

[ ]

[ ]

[ ]

Name:

✝ _____

✝ _____

✝ _____

✝ _____

Message:

Name:

✝ _____

✝ _____

✝ _____

✝ _____

Message:

Name:

✝ _____

✝ _____

✝ _____

✝ _____

Message:

[ ]

[ ]

[ ]

[ ]

Name:

✝ _____

✝ _____

✝ _____

✝ _____

Message:

Name:

Message:

† _____

† _____

† _____

† _____

Made in United States
North Haven, CT
04 May 2023

36264275R00057